Planetary Pot

Planetary Pot

ALIGNING WITH
ASTROLOGICAL HERBS

Matthew Petchinsky

Apophis Enterprises LLC

1

⁓

Planetary Pot: Aligning with Astrological Herbs: Volume 1
By: Matthew Petchinsky

Introduction: The Cosmic Connection to Herbalism

In the serene tapestry of the cosmos, where stars gleam with ancient secrets and planets trace their silent orbits, there lies a profound and often overlooked connection to the earthly realm of flora. "Planetary Pot: Aligning with Astrological Herbs: Volume 1" invites you on a celestial journey that intertwines the mystic allure of astrology with the grounded, healing presence of herbalism. This connection, rooted in the wisdom of the ancients, holds the key to enhancing our use of herbs for healing, wellness, and spiritual growth. By exploring this symbiotic relationship, we uncover new dimensions of understanding both the cosmos and the natural world.

The purpose of this book is not merely to present an encyclopedic knowledge of herbs and their astrological correspondences but to guide you through a transformative process of learning, application, and reflection. We delve into the astrological associations of various herbs to unveil how celestial forces can influence and enhance their properties. This knowledge, when applied, offers a powerful tool for those seeking to harness the energies of the universe in their pursuit of wellness and self-discovery.

As we embark on this journey together, you can expect to uncover practical applications that bring the power of these astrological herbs into your daily life. Through a blend of historical insights, practical tips, and guided exercises, this book aims to illuminate the path to a deeper connection with the natural world through the lens of the stars. Each chapter is designed to align with specific planetary energies, providing a structured yet flexible approach to exploring herbalism within the cosmic framework.

Prepare to expand your understanding of herbal properties through the rich context of astrology, exploring how plants like the bold sunflower resonate with the Sun's vibrant energy or how the reflective moon influences the soothing powers of moonwort. This book promises to be an enlightening guide, offering a comprehensive view of how ancient wisdom can inform modern practices, leading to a more harmonious and spiritually aligned way of living.

Let "Planetary Pot: Aligning with Astrological Herbs: Volume 1" be your guide as you navigate the vast universe of herbal wisdom, finding your footing among the stars and learning to draw upon their ancient power to enrich and elevate your herbal practice.

Chapter 1: Foundations of Astrological Herbalism
Astrology and Herbalism: A Historical Integration

The confluence of astrology and herbalism is a tapestry woven through time, intricately linked by cultures that observed the cosmos for deeper meaning and guidance. This union finds its origins in ancient civilizations where the movements of celestial bodies were believed to directly influence the physical and spiritual realms. Historical documents and practices from societies such as the Egyptians, Greeks, Chinese, and Indians provide profound insights into how astrology shaped herbal medicine.

In ancient Egypt, priests who were also physicians prescribed herbal remedies based on planetary alignments. Similarly, in Greece, the legendary physician Hippocrates, often called the "Father of Medicine," incorporated astrological principles into his herbal prescriptions, asserting that one must understand the patterns of the stars to truly grasp the art of healing.

The Ayurvedic traditions of India meticulously categorized herbs according to the energies of the planets and the doshas (body constitutions) they could balance. Chinese medicine too saw a parallel approach, where the energy (Qi) of plants was used to harmonize with the elemental energies believed to be influenced by celestial dynamics.

Through these practices, it becomes evident that across different eras and civilizations, there was a shared belief in the celestial influence over herbal efficacy. This historical backdrop sets the stage for understanding how modern astrological herbalism can be both a continuation and a refinement of these ancient wisdoms.

Basic Principles of Astrology in Herbalism

To fully engage with astrological herbalism, one must grasp some fundamental astrological concepts that form the backbone of this discipline. These include:

- **Planets**: Each planet exerts its own unique influence on herbal properties. For instance, Mars might enhance the potency of spices that invigorate the blood, whereas Venus could soften and harmonize through flowers and fruits.
- **Signs**: The zodiac signs provide a context for how herbs manifest their characteristics. Herbs associated with Scorpio, a water sign, may be potent in detoxifying, reflecting the sign's association with transformation and healing.
- **Houses**: The astrological houses relate to different life areas and can guide herbal applications. Herbs that fall into the 6th house, for example, might be particularly effective for daily health routines.
- **Aspects**: The angles planets make to one another can affect the way their energies combine or clash, which in turn influences how combined herbal properties might behave.

Understanding these elements allows practitioners to select herbs not only for their physical properties but also for their astrological resonance, enhancing the healing and transformative potential of herbal remedies.

Herbal Basics: Understanding the Craft

Before delving into astrological specifics, it is essential to have a solid foundation in herbalism. This includes understanding the different parts of plants used in herbal medicine:

- **Leaves and Flowers**: Often used for their quick-acting effects in teas or tinctures.
- **Roots and Barks**: Typically used in treatments requiring slow, sustained release of plant properties.
- **Seeds and Berries**: Commonly used for their concentrated energies and potent therapeutic properties.

In terms of preparation, herbs can be utilized in various forms, including teas, tinctures, capsules, oils, and salves. Each method extracts different types of compounds from the herbs, and choosing the right preparation can enhance the herb's effectiveness and alignment with astrological influences.

Safety is paramount in herbalism. It's crucial to understand not only the potential healing properties of herbs but also their contraindications and the importance of dosage. Just as one would respect the power of the celestial bodies, so too must one respect the power inherent in each plant.

Conclusion

This foundational knowledge of both astrology and herbalism creates a framework through which we can explore deeper, more nuanced applications of herbs aligned with astrological principles. As we continue in "Planetary Pot: Aligning with Astrological Herbs: Volume 1," we will build upon these basics to more advanced techniques that integrate celestial wisdom with herbal practice, guiding you towards a harmonious balance between the cosmos and the natural world.

If you are looking for the best deals and quick and discreet shipping, head over to my virtual dispensary:
https://shift.store/sg1fan23477/retail

Now, there are many unique items from hemp buds, to smoke buds to infused drinks.

Chapter 2: The Sun and Its Herbs

Solar Influence: The Heartbeat of Vitality and Energy

The Sun, in both astrology and herbalism, is synonymous with life force, vitality, and the core essence of being. In astrology, the Sun represents our identity, ego, and the vital energies that drive our ambition and will to live. It influences growth, health, and prosperity, radiating its force to animate the natural world. In the realm of plants, the Sun is equally pivotal; it is essential for photosynthesis, the process by which plants convert light to energy, and thus sustains all life on Earth.

In herbalism, Sun-associated herbs typically carry qualities of warmth, invigoration, and healing, especially of the spirit and mood. They are often used to address issues of the heart and mind, promote healthy circulation, and support the immune system. These herbs tend to embody the Sun's properties of bringing cheer, brightness, and strength.

Key Herbs of the Sun

St. John's Wort (Hypericum perforatum)

Description and Uses: St. John's Wort is a perennial herb known for its vibrant yellow flowers, which seem to capture the essence of sunlight. Traditionally, it has been used to ward off evil spirits and is renowned in modern herbalism for its antidepressant qualities. It is often prescribed for mild to moderate depression, seasonal affective disorder, and anxiety. Its medicinal components include hypericin and hyperforin, which are thought to affect neurotransmitters in the brain related to mood regulation.

Astrological Significance: Astrologically, St. John's Wort is linked with the Sun and is believed to be most potent when harvested at Midsummer, during the Sun's peak strength. This herb embodies the Sun's power to banish darkness and illuminate the inner workings of the mind, making it a powerful ally against mental shadows.

Calendula (Calendula officinalis)

Description and Uses: Calendula, with its golden blooms, is another Sun-associated herb that exudes the solar qualities of healing and protection. It is extensively used in topical applications to soothe skin irritations, heal cuts and wounds, and improve skin health. Calendula is antifungal, anti-inflammatory, and antibacterial, making it an excellent herb for salves and creams to treat skin conditions.

Astrological Significance: Calendula's connection to the Sun extends beyond its bright appearance to its healing capabilities, which are thought to be enhanced when the plant is exposed to robust sunlight. In astrology, Calendula is used to invoke solar energy for protection and to strengthen the individual's vitality, reinforcing the skin as a barrier against physical and energetic harm.

Other Notable Sun Herbs

- **Sunflower (Helianthus annuus):** True to its name, the sunflower is not only visually reminiscent of the Sun but also follows the sunlight throughout the day in young buds, a phenomenon known as heliotropism. Sunflower seeds are nutritious, and the oil is beneficial for the skin and heart, embodying the Sun's nourishing qualities.
- **Lemon Balm (Melissa officinalis):** This herb is known for its uplifting and soothing properties. It enhances mood, aids digestion,

and can help relieve stress and anxiety, mirroring the Sun's ability to brighten and stabilize.

- **Angelica (Angelica archangelica):** Traditionally used to purify and protect, Angelica is said to harness the protective qualities of the Sun. It is used in treating colds and flu and is believed to warm and fortify the body.

Conclusion

In this chapter, we have explored how the Sun's astrological significance translates into the herbal world, providing us with plants that embody its energy of light, warmth, and vitality. These Sun-associated herbs not only offer practical health benefits but also carry deeper symbolic meanings, helping us align more closely with the solar qualities of radiance, strength, and life force. As we integrate these herbs into our practices, we draw upon the Sun's profound energy, enhancing our own wellness and vitality.

If you are looking for the best deals and quick and discreet shipping, head over to my virtual dispensary:

https://shift.store/sg1fan23477/retail

Chapter 3: The Moon and Its Herbs

Lunar Properties: Influence Over Emotional and Physical Health

The Moon, with its mystical and ethereal presence, casts a profound influence on both the emotional and physical realms of human experience. In astrology, the Moon governs emotions, intuition, and the subconscious, as well as aspects of our physical health related to rhythms, cycles, and fluids in the body. It reflects our deepest needs and our way of reacting and adapting to our environment. The Moon's phases themselves—waxing, full, waning, and new—mirror the natural cycles of growth, culmination, release, and renewal that we experience in our lives.

Herbally, plants associated with the Moon often have properties that support the emotional and fluidic systems of the body, including the lymphatic and hormonal systems. They tend to promote calming, soothing, and nurturing effects, making them ideal for addressing issues of stress, anxiety, and other emotional disturbances, as well as supporting reproductive health and fluid balance.

Key Herbs of the Moon

Jasmine (Jasminum officinale)

Description and Uses: Jasmine, with its intoxicatingly sweet fragrance, is traditionally used to calm the nerves and uplift the spirits. It is often employed in teas and essential oils for its relaxing properties, which are particularly useful in combating stress and insomnia. Jasmine tea is a well-known relaxant, and its essential oil is often used in aromatherapy to enhance mood and alleviate emotional distress.

Astrological Significance: In astrology, Jasmine is connected with the Moon, enhancing its ability to soothe the emotional body and help align one's inner rhythms with the natural world. The sweet, almost hypnotic fragrance of Jasmine is particularly aligned with the Moon's power to influence the subconscious and nurture the psyche, making it a perfect herb for meditation and relaxation practices during the evening when the Moon is prominent.

White Willow (Salix alba)

Description and Uses: White Willow bark, the original source of salicylic acid (the basis for aspirin), has been used for centuries to relieve pain and reduce fever. It is particularly effective in treating headaches, muscle pain, and rheumatic conditions. As a natural anti-inflammatory, it is gentler on the stomach than its synthetic descendants, making it a preferred choice for natural pain management.

Astrological Significance: Aligned with the Moon due to its soothing, calming properties and its affinity with water, White Willow exemplifies the lunar qualities of flow and adaptability. It is particularly resonant with the Moon's ability to ease transitions and smooth out emotional and physical imbalances.

Other Notable Moon Herbs

- **Mugwort (Artemisia vulgaris):** Traditionally used for its dream-enhancing and digestive properties, Mugwort is deeply connected to the Moon's mystical influence. It is often used in protective sachets and dream pillows to enhance psychic dreams and astral travel.
- **Water Lily (Nymphaea odorata):** The serene water lily, growing in calm waters, symbolizes the Moon's dominion over fluids and emotional peace. It is used to calm the nerves and soothe the heart, reflecting the Moon's tranquil and reflective nature.
- **Camphor (Cinnamomum camphora):** Known for its cooling and refreshing scent, Camphor is used to relieve pain and reduce fever, similar to White Willow. Its clear, penetrating qualities capture the Moon's ability to clarify and cleanse the emotional and physical planes.

Conclusion

In this chapter, we have explored the Moon's influence over our emotional and physical health through its herbal correspondences. The herbs discussed here not only offer therapeutic properties that align with the Moon's nurturing and soothing energies but also serve as tools to connect more deeply with the lunar cycles and their impact on our lives. By integrating these Moon herbs into our practices, we embrace the Moon's capacity to heal, refresh, and transform, enhancing our well-being in alignment with the natural rhythms of the universe.

If you are looking for the best deals and quick and discreet shipping, head over to my virtual dispensary:
https://shift.store/sg1fan23477/retail

Chapter 4: Mercury and Its Herbs

Mercurial Traits: Master of Communication and Mental Agility

Mercury, often depicted as the fleet-footed messenger of the gods in mythology, holds dominion over communication, intellect, and the exchange of information in astrology. This planet influences how we think, learn, communicate, and process information. It's the driving force behind our reasoning capabilities, our ability to express ourselves, and how we connect with others on a cerebral level. Mercury's energy is quick, alert, and often restless, mirroring the constant motion and flow of ideas and words.

In the realm of herbalism, Mercury-associated herbs typically enhance cognitive functions, support the nervous system, and aid in communication. These herbs can sharpen the mind, ease nervous tension, and help improve both verbal and non-verbal communication. They are particularly beneficial during times when clear thinking, concentration, and effective communication are needed.

Key Herbs of Mercury

Lavender (Lavandula angustifolia)

Description and Uses: Lavender is renowned for its soothing scent and its ability to calm the mind and ease anxiety. It's often used in aromatherapy to reduce stress and promote relaxation, which can help clear the mind for better decision-making and communication. Lavender oil is also used to enhance sleep quality, thereby supporting cognitive functions by ensuring the mind is rested and rejuvenated.

Astrological Significance: Aligned with Mercury, Lavender supports clear communication by calming nervous anxiety that can cloud thoughts. Its soothing properties help to stabilize the mental state, promoting a serene environment from which thoughts can flow more freely and communication can be more effective.

Rosemary (Rosmarinus officinalis)

Description and Uses: Rosemary is often associated with remembrance and cognitive enhancement. It has been traditionally used to improve memory, focus, and overall brain health. Studies have suggested that inhaling Rosemary essential oil can help increase concentration and memory, making it an excellent herb for studying or engaging in tasks that require sustained mental effort.

Astrological Significance: Rosemary's connection to Mercury lies in its ability to bolster the mental faculties that Mercury governs. The herb enhances mental clarity and focus, aiding in the quick and agile thinking that is characteristic of Mercurial energy. It is particularly beneficial when Mercury is retrograde, a period known for communication mishaps and information breakdowns.

Other Notable Mercury Herbs

- **Peppermint (Mentha piperita):** Peppermint is invigorating to the mind and can help improve concentration and mental alertness. Its refreshing scent is ideal for clearing mental fog, making it a favorite during long working hours or study sessions.
- **Lemon Balm (Melissa officinalis):** Known for its calming effects, Lemon Balm can alleviate stress and anxiety, which improves communication by easing the mind and allowing for smoother interaction in social and professional settings.
- **Echinacea (Echinacea spp.):** Traditionally used to boost the immune system, Echinacea also supports throat health, which can be crucial for clear verbal communication, aligning well with Mercury's domain over expression and dialogue.

Conclusion

In this chapter, we've explored Mercury's pivotal role in enhancing intellectual and communicative abilities through its herbal correspondents. Herbs like Lavender and Rosemary not only support the cognitive functions governed by Mercury but also facilitate the clear and effective communication that Mercury enhances. Integrating these herbs into daily practices can significantly improve mental agility and communicative abilities, making them invaluable tools for those seeking to harness the power of Mercury in their personal and professional lives.

If you are looking for the best deals and quick and discreet shipping, head over to my virtual dispensary:

https://shift.store/sg1fan23477/retail

Chapter 5: Venus and Its Herbs

Venusian Attributes: Governess of Love, Beauty, and Relationships

Venus, celebrated in both mythology and astrology as the embodiment of love, beauty, and harmony, casts a profound influence on our interpersonal relationships, our sense of aesthetics, and our pursuit of pleasure. In the astrological realm, Venus governs how we express affection, attract others, and experience joy and satisfaction in our lives. It also plays a crucial role in personal self-esteem and the appreciation of beauty both in oneself and in the environment.

Herbs associated with Venus often possess qualities that enhance beauty, promote emotional well-being, and support heart health. These plants typically have a pleasing appearance and aroma, and their healing properties are often employed in ways that harmonize and enhance both physical attractiveness and inner balance.

Key Herbs of Venus

Rose (Rosa spp.)

Description and Uses: The rose, with its iconic beauty and alluring fragrance, is a quintessential symbol of love and is deeply connected to Venusian energy. Roses are used extensively in skincare products for their hydrating and soothing properties, which help improve skin tone and texture. Rosewater and rose essential oil are popular in beauty treatments to promote a youthful complexion and calm irritated skin. Internally, rose tea can uplift the spirit and soothe the heart, helping to ease emotional stress and mend a broken heart.

Astrological Significance: The connection between roses and Venus is emblematic of the planet's influence on beauty and love. The rose's ability to heal the emotional body and enhance physical beauty aligns perfectly with Venus's domain over love and aesthetics, making it an essential herb in any Venusian practice.

Hibiscus (Hibiscus rosa-sinensis)

Description and Uses: Hibiscus, known for its vibrant, trumpet-shaped flowers, is commonly used in teas and natural health products for its beneficial effects on cardiovascular health. It helps to lower blood pressure and maintain healthy cholesterol levels, which are vital for heart health. Hibiscus is also rich in antioxidants and can help to promote a healthy complexion, making it a favorite in beauty treatments for its anti-aging properties.

Astrological Significance: The hibiscus flower's ties to Venus are found in its striking appearance and its capacity to foster heart health and emotional well-being. Its role in promoting both internal and external beauty and in nurturing the heart chakra makes it a powerful ally for those working with Venusian energies.

Other Notable Venus Herbs

- **Vanilla (Vanilla planifolia):** With its sweet, enchanting fragrance, vanilla is often used in perfumery and flavoring, enhancing sensory pleasure and comfort. Its association with Venus underscores its use in cultivating sweetness in relationships and attracting joyful experiences.
- **Jasmine (Jasminum officinale):** Known for its seductive scent, Jasmine is traditionally used to balance hormones and promote skin health. It aligns with Venus through its role in enhancing romantic feelings and beautifying the environment.
- **Tarragon (Artemisia dracunculus):** Often called the "King of Herbs" in French cuisine, tarragon aids digestion and stimulates

the appetite for life, mirroring Venus's influence on pleasure and satisfaction in both culinary and social settings.

Conclusion

This chapter delves into the profound influence of Venus on the herbal kingdom, showcasing plants that epitomize love, beauty, and relational harmony. By incorporating these Venus-associated herbs into our daily routines, we can enhance our connection to Venusian qualities, enriching our relationships, beautifying our surroundings, and fostering an overall sense of well-being and joy in our lives.

If you are looking for the best deals and quick and discreet shipping, head over to my virtual dispensary:

https://shift.store/sg1fan23477/retail

Chapter 6: Mars and Its Herbs

Martial Aspects: Energy, Courage, and Conflict

Mars, often revered as the god of war in mythology, is the planet associated with energy, aggression, courage, and conflict in astrology. It governs our capacity to assert ourselves, our stamina, and our ability to confront and overcome challenges. Mars influences our physical energy and vitality, driving us to action and enabling us to execute our ambitions and protect ourselves in times of need.

In the realm of herbalism, Mars-associated herbs are typically invigorating, stimulating, and protective. They are often used to boost energy, enhance physical strength, and support the immune system. Additionally, these herbs can have warming and spicy characteristics, reflecting Mars' fiery nature.

Key Herbs of Mars

Garlic (Allium sativum)

Description and Uses: Garlic, with its potent flavor and powerful medicinal properties, is a staple in culinary and medicinal practices worldwide. It is renowned for its immune-boosting effects, helping to fight off infections and maintain healthy circulation. Garlic is also used to enhance endurance and vitality, making it a popular supplement among athletes and those looking to sustain high energy levels throughout the day.

Astrological Significance: Garlic's association with Mars stems from its ability to act as a natural antibiotic and its robust, penetrating qualities that mirror Mars' attributes of protection and strength. It embodies the martial energy of warding off illness and enhancing the body's resilience, making it an essential herb for those looking to harness Mars' vigorous and protective energy.

Ginger (Zingiber officinale)

Description and Uses: Ginger is a powerful herb known for its stimulating and warming properties. It aids digestion, alleviates nausea, and reduces inflammation, making it a versatile remedy in both culinary and medicinal contexts. Ginger's ability to boost circulation and relieve pain also makes it a valuable herb for improving overall energy levels and supporting muscle recovery.

Astrological Significance: The warming and energizing nature of ginger corresponds with Mars' fiery and dynamic essence. It supports Mars' themes of action and initiation by enhancing physical vitality and stimulating the body's internal fire, which is crucial for maintaining an active and healthy lifestyle.

Other Notable Mars Herbs

- **Cayenne (Capsicum annuum):** Known for its hot and spicy flavor, cayenne pepper is a circulatory stimulant that can boost metabolism and improve heart health. Its fiery nature makes it a quintessential Mars herb, ideal for invigorating the body and spirit.
- **Basil (Ocimum basilicum):** Basil enhances vigor and is believed

to promote courage and wealth, aligning well with Mars' influence on drive and determination. It is also used to treat various digestive and inflammatory disorders, reflecting Mars' protective qualities.

- **Nettle (Urtica dioica):** Nettle is a fortifying herb, rich in nutrients and known for its ability to support joint health and improve energy levels. Its stinging properties, which defend the plant from predators, mirror Mars' protective and combative nature.

Conclusion

This chapter has explored Mars and its associated herbs, highlighting how these plants can be utilized to embody the energy, courage, and protective strength characteristic of Mars. By incorporating these Mars herbs into our health regimen, we tap into their robust qualities, enhancing our physical vitality and empowering us to tackle challenges with confidence and resilience.

If you are looking for the best deals and quick and discreet shipping, head over to my virtual dispensary:

https://shift.store/sg1fan23477/retail

Chapter 7: Jupiter and Its Herbs

Jovian Impact: Expansion, Prosperity, and Protection

Jupiter, the largest planet in our solar system, is known in astrology as the great benefactor, bringing expansion, optimism, luck, and abundance. Its influence extends to growth, both spiritual and material, and it encourages us to seek knowledge, truth, and deeper understanding. Jupiter's expansive nature also relates to protection and the warding off of negativity, making it a powerful ally in seeking both personal and communal well-being.

Herbs associated with Jupiter often share these expansive qualities and are used to promote growth, prosperity, health, and protection. These plants typically possess robust flavors or significant medicinal properties that enhance physical and spiritual abundance.

Key Herbs of Jupiter

Sage (Salvia officinalis)

Description and Uses: Sage is a revered herb known for its culinary and medicinal properties. It has been used traditionally to ward off evil, promote wisdom, and enhance memory. In medicine, sage is recognized for its antiseptic, anti-inflammatory, and digestive properties. It is also used to help alleviate sore throats, boost cognitive function, and regulate digestion.

Astrological Significance: Sage's association with Jupiter lies in its capacity to protect and to expand the mind and spirit. As a herb of wisdom and protection, sage embodies Jupiter's themes of growth and safeguarding well-being. Its use in cleansing rituals, where it is burned to purify spaces of negative energy, also reflects Jupiter's role in promoting spiritual prosperity and protection.

Dandelion (Taraxacum officinale)

Description and Uses: Often regarded as a simple weed, dandelion is a powerhouse of nutrition, packed with vitamins and minerals. It is used to cleanse the liver, promote digestive health, and support overall detoxification in the body. Dandelion's diuretic properties make it excellent for reducing water retention and purifying the blood.

Astrological Significance: Dandelion reflects Jupiter's influence through its ability to promote physical growth and health, symbolizing prosperity and survival. The plant's robust nature, thriving in diverse environments, mirrors Jupiter's themes of expansion and adaptability. Its role in cleansing and regeneration aligns with Jupiter's association with healing and protection.

Other Notable Jupiter Herbs

- **Cinnamon (Cinnamomum verum):** Cinnamon is used to attract success and healing. Its sweet, warm properties stimulate the circulatory system, aiding in the expansion of energy and health, which are key aspects of Jupiter's beneficial influence.
- **Turmeric (Curcuma longa):** Known for its potent anti-inflammatory and antioxidant properties, turmeric promotes health and longevity, reflecting Jupiter's life-enhancing qualities. It is also used in rituals to bring about prosperity and to cleanse the energy of a space.
- **Milk Thistle (Silybum marianum):** Milk thistle is best known for its protective effects on the liver, an organ associated with growth and regeneration. Its silymarin content helps to repair liver cells and protect against toxins, embodying Jupiter's protective and healing energy.

Conclusion

In this chapter, we have explored Jupiter's grand role in promoting expansion, prosperity, and protection through its associated herbs. These plants not only enhance our physical and spiritual growth but also align us with Jupiter's benevolent energies, helping us to attract abundance and safeguard our well-being. By incorporating Jupiter's herbs into our practices, we invite the planet's generous and protective qualities into our lives, fostering a sense of richness and expansiveness in all we do.

If you are looking for the best deals and quick and discreet shipping, head over to my virtual dispensary:

https://shift.store/sg1fan23477/retail

Chapter 8: Saturn and Its Herbs

Saturnine Principles: Discipline, Restrictions, and Longevity

Saturn, often depicted as the taskmaster of the planets, governs discipline, responsibility, and restrictions. It represents time, longevity, and endurance, teaching us the importance of structure, hard work, and perseverance. Saturn's influence is felt in life's challenges and the lessons we learn through overcoming them. In astrology, Saturn helps us develop resilience and wisdom, often through trials and hardships, shaping our character and life path.

Herbs associated with Saturn often have properties that reflect its principles of protection, healing, and long-term preservation. These herbs are typically robust, offering deep, foundational healing rather than quick fixes. They can help fortify the body against the stresses and strains of life, embodying Saturn's qualities of endurance and resilience.

Key Herbs of Saturn

Comfrey (Symphytum officinale)

Description and Uses: Comfrey, known for its remarkable healing properties, particularly in mending bones and tissues, is a powerful Saturnine herb. It contains allantoin, a substance that helps regenerate cell growth, making it invaluable in healing sprains, bruises, fractures, and wounds. Comfrey is used topically in poultices and salves to treat injuries and reduce inflammation, aiding the body's natural healing processes.

Astrological Significance: Comfrey's association with Saturn is evident in its deep healing abilities, reflecting Saturn's themes of recovery and regeneration. It promotes the long-term healing and strengthening of the body, much like Saturn encourages us to develop inner strength and resilience over time.

Kava (Piper methysticum)

Description and Uses: Kava is known for its calming and soothing effects on the nervous system, making it a popular herb for relieving anxiety, stress, and insomnia. It creates a sense of well-being, eases pain, and relaxes muscles, without diminishing cognitive function. Kava is used both ceremonially and therapeutically to foster a calm and focused state, ideal for deep contemplation and meditation.

Astrological Significance: Kava's soothing properties reflect Saturn's role in fostering discipline and focus, providing the mental clarity needed to face Saturn's challenges. It helps mitigate the stress associated with Saturn's tests and restrictions, offering protection for the mind and spirit during times of hardship.

Other Notable Saturn Herbs

- **Horsetail (Equisetum arvense):** Rich in silica, horsetail helps in strengthening bones, hair, and nails, aligning with Saturn's association with structure and longevity. It is also used for its diuretic properties, helping to cleanse the system of toxins, thereby embodying Saturn's principle of purification through challenge.
- **Skullcap (Scutellaria lateriflora):** This herb is beneficial for stabilizing emotions and reducing anxiety, useful in managing the mental and emotional stress that can come with Saturn's lessons. It promotes endurance and resilience, key Saturnine qualities.
- **Slippery Elm (Ulmus rubra):** Known for its soothing mucilage, slippery elm protects and heals mucous membranes, and is used in treating digestive issues, another aspect of the foundational and protective qualities associated with Saturn.

Conclusion

In this chapter, we have delved into Saturn's connection with discipline, restriction, and longevity, exploring how Saturnine herbs like Comfrey and Kava embody these principles through their healing and protective properties. These herbs support our physical, emotional, and spiritual fortitude, helping us to navigate Saturn's challenges with resilience and wisdom. By incorporating Saturn-associated herbs into our practices, we align ourselves with the planet's stabilizing energy, fostering endurance and strength to face life's hurdles.

If you are looking for the best deals and quick and discreet shipping, head over to my virtual dispensary:

https://shift.store/sg1fan23477/retail

Chapter 9: Uranus, Neptune, and Pluto: The Outer Planets and Their Herbs

Ethereal Influences: Mystical and Transformative Properties

The outer planets—Uranus, Neptune, and Pluto—each play a profound role in the deeper, often unseen forces of life. These planets influence our innovation, intuition, and transformation at both personal and collective levels. Their slow orbits mean their effects are felt over generations, molding societal shifts and personal revolutions.

- **Uranus** is the planet of sudden changes, revolutions, and breakthroughs. It disrupts the status quo with innovative ideas and technologies, pushing us toward progress and awakening.
- **Neptune** governs the realm of dreams, intuition, and psychic sensitivity. It dissolves boundaries, enhancing empathy and our connection to the spiritual and unseen world.
- **Pluto** represents transformation, power, and rebirth. It deals with the subconscious forces, including death and regeneration, pushing us to confront our deepest selves and evolve.

Herbs associated with these planets often possess unique and potent properties that can help us harness their ethereal and transformative energies. These plants may be less common in traditional herbalism but offer profound spiritual and psychological benefits.

Key Herbs of Uranus, Neptune, and Pluto

Mugwort (Artemisia vulgaris) – Uranus

Description and Uses: Mugwort is renowned for its association with dreams and psychic vision, making it a fitting herb for Uranus's influence on awakening and enlightenment. It is used to stimulate the psyche, enhance lucid dreaming, and as a protective herb during spiritual exploration.

Astrological Significance: Mugwort's ability to open the mind to new psychic experiences and dimensions aligns closely with Uranus's role as the harbinger of change and innovation, especially in the spiritual realm.

Blue Lotus (Nymphaea caerulea) – Neptune

Description and Uses: The blue lotus was revered in ancient Egypt for its seductive scent and psychoactive properties, believed to provide relief from pain, increase memory, and promote sexual desire. It is often used in tea, incense, and essential oil form to enhance meditation, induce deep relaxation, and foster spiritual connection.

Astrological Significance: Blue Lotus exemplifies Neptune's control over the mystical and ethereal, facilitating deeper understanding and connection to the spiritual aspects of life, enhancing intuition, and dissolving the usual mental boundaries.

Belladonna (Atropa belladonna) – Pluto

Description and Uses: Also known as deadly nightshade, Belladonna is a powerful and dangerous herb used historically in small doses to relieve pain, muscle spasms, and inflammation. Due to its toxic nature, it is rarely used in modern herbalism without professional guidance but is noted for its profound effects on the nervous system and as a potent hallucinogen.

Astrological Significance: Belladonna's potent properties of transformation and its association with death and rebirth mirror Pluto's influence. It embodies Pluto's transformative power, urging profound internal shifts and awakening deeper subconscious truths.

Other Notable Outer Planet Herbs

- **Salvia divinorum (Sage of the Diviners) – Neptune:** Used by the Mazatec shamans for visionary states in healing rituals, it facilitates spiritual journeys and deep introspection, aligning with Neptune's ethereal essence.
- **Hawthorn (Crataegus) – Pluto:** Often used in traditional medicine to support heart health and emotional healing, Hawthorn can aid in personal transformation and renewal, reflecting Pluto's themes of death and rebirth.

Conclusion

In this chapter, we explored the mystical and transformative influences of the outer planets and introduced some unique herbs associated with Uranus, Neptune, and Pluto. These herbs, though less common, offer powerful ways to engage with the deep, often challenging energies of these distant celestial bodies. By understanding and integrating these potent plants into our practices, we can harness the innovative, intuitive, and transformative powers of the outer planets, aiding our spiritual growth and personal evolution.

If you are looking for the best deals and quick and discreet shipping, head over to my virtual dispensary:

https://shift.store/sg1fan23477/retail

Conclusion: Integrating Astrological Wisdom with Herbal Practice

As we conclude our journey through "Planetary Pot: Aligning with Astrological Herbs: Volume 1," we reflect on the rich tapestry of insights that connect the celestial influences of the planets with the earthly wisdom of herbs. Each chapter has unveiled specific planetary energies and their corresponding herbal associations, providing a deep understanding of how these elements interact to influence our health, well-being, and spiritual growth.

Summary of Planetary Insights and Herbal Associations

- **The Sun**: Herbs like St. John's Wort and Calendula reflect the Sun's vibrant energy, enhancing vitality and promoting healing, particularly in terms of mental health and skin care.
- **The Moon**: Jasmine and White Willow embody the Moon's soothing, reflective qualities, offering support for emotional balance and physical fluidity, crucial for managing stress and maintaining personal harmony.
- **Mercury**: Herbs such as Lavender and Rosemary enhance Mercury's influence on communication and cognitive function, aiding in clarity of thought and ease of expression.
- **Venus**: With Rose and Hibiscus, we tap into Venus's realm of beauty and love, utilizing these herbs to nurture heart health and enhance physical and emotional allure.
- **Mars**: Energizing herbs like Garlic and Ginger resonate with Mars's

dynamic energy, boosting vitality and providing protection against physical ailments.

- **Jupiter**: Sage and Dandelion expand Jupiter's themes of growth and prosperity, supporting bodily health and spiritual abundance.
- **Saturn**: Resilient herbs such as Comfrey and Kava reflect Saturn's grounding and enduring qualities, helping to build inner strength and promote healing.
- **Uranus, Neptune, and Pluto**: Uncommon herbs like Mugwort, Blue Lotus, and Belladonna link us to the transformational and transcendent energies of the outer planets, guiding deep spiritual explorations and profound change.

Practical Application: Bringing the Heavens to Earth

Encouraged by the knowledge gained, you are now equipped to integrate these astrological and herbal insights into your daily health and wellness routines. Start by identifying personal needs aligned with specific planetary energies. For instance, incorporate Sun-associated herbs to enhance vitality during winter months, or use Mercury-related herbs to support communication skills during important discussions or projects.

Herbal practices can also be synchronized with the lunar cycle, utilizing Moon herbs to reflect and reset emotionally each month. Creating tinctures, teas, or capsules according to astrological timings can maximize the efficacy of these herbs, making your practice both a science and an art.

Future Directions: Expanding Horizons

As you continue to explore astrological herbalism, consider keeping a journal of your experiences with different planetary herbs and their effects on your body, mind, and spirit. This personalized record can guide you in refining and adapting your practices to better suit your evolving needs and circumstances.

Further education through workshops, courses, or reading can deepen your understanding and proficiency. Engaging with a community of like-minded individuals can provide support and inspire new ideas, enhancing your journey in astrological herbalism.

Lastly, experiment with growing your own astrological herbs. Cultivating these plants not only deepens your connection to their energy but also ensures you have a fresh, potent supply for your practice.

Closing Thoughts

"Planetary Pot: Aligning with Astrological Herbs: Volume 1" has aimed to illuminate the path where the stars align with the soil. By weaving together the ancient arts of astrology and herbalism, we not only honor these traditions but also open ourselves to a more interconnected and holistic approach to wellness. As you continue to align with the cosmic flow through the wise use of herbs, may you find balance, health, and profound satisfaction in your practice.

Appendix A: Herbal Preparations and Recipes

In "Planetary Pot: Aligning with Astrological Herbs: Volume 1," we explore the connection between celestial influences and herbal practices. This appendix provides practical guidelines on preparing herbal formulations, along with specific recipes to integrate the power of astrological herbs into your daily life. These preparations and recipes aim to enhance both health and spiritual well-being, harnessing the unique energies discussed throughout the book.

Preparation Techniques

1. **Tinctures**
   - **Materials Needed**: Fresh or dried herbs, high-proof alcohol (such as vodka or brandy), a clean jar with a lid, and a strainer.
   - **Instructions**:

   1. Fill the jar ⅓ full with dried herbs or ½ full with fresh herbs.

2. Pour alcohol over the herbs until completely submerged, and leave an inch of alcohol above the herbs to account for expansion.
3. Seal the jar and store it in a cool, dark place for 4-6 weeks, shaking it daily.
4. After the infusion period, strain the herbs out using a cheesecloth or fine mesh, squeezing out as much liquid as possible.
5. Store the tincture in amber dropper bottles for easy use. Label each bottle with the herb and date of preparation.

2. **Herbal Teas**
   - **Materials Needed**: Dried herbs, tea infuser or teapot, boiling water.
   - **Instructions**:

1. Boil water and allow it to cool slightly to just below boiling temperature.
2. Add about 1 teaspoon of dried herbs per cup of water into the tea infuser or teapot.
3. Pour hot water over the herbs and cover to steep. Let it steep for 5-10 minutes, depending on the desired strength.
4. Strain and enjoy. Sweeten with honey or lemon if desired.

3. **Salves**
   - **Materials Needed**: Herbs, carrier oil (such as coconut or olive oil), beeswax, double boiler, and storage containers.
   - **Instructions**:

1. Infuse the carrier oil with herbs either by heating them together in a double boiler for 2-3 hours on low heat or by letting the herbs sit in the oil in a sunny spot for 2-3 weeks.
2. Strain the herbs from the oil using cheesecloth.
3. Heat the infused oil in a double boiler and add beeswax (about ¼ ounce beeswax per cup of oil). Stir until melted and well combined.

4. Pour the mixture into clean storage containers and let it cool until solid.

Recipes for Health and Spiritual Well-Being

1. Sun Vitality Tea
- **Ingredients**: 1 part St. John's Wort, 1 part Calendula, 1 part Lemon balm.
- **Instructions**: Blend the herbs and steep in hot water for 10 minutes. Drink daily in the morning to invoke the energizing power of the Sun for vitality and clarity.

2. Moonlit Calming Tincture
- **Ingredients**: Equal parts Jasmine and White Willow bark.
- **Instructions**: Follow the tincture preparation method. Use 1-2 droppers full in water or tea before bedtime to enhance emotional balance and promote restful sleep under the influence of the Moon.

3. Mercury Focus Salve
- **Ingredients**: Rosemary infused oil, Peppermint essential oil, beeswax.
- **Instructions**: Prepare a salve using the infused Rosemary oil, add a few drops of Peppermint essential oil during the beeswax melting stage. Apply to temples and wrists when needing clarity and concentration.

4. Venus Beauty Bath
- **Ingredients**: Rose petals, Hibiscus flowers, Epsom salts.
- **Instructions**: Mix the ingredients and add to a warm bath. Soak for 20 minutes to harness Venus's properties for skin beauty and emotional soothing.

5. **Mars Energy Booster**
   * **Ingredients**: Ginger, Cayenne pepper.
   * **Instructions**: Prepare a tincture using these herbs. Add a few drops to warm water or tea in the morning to kick-start your day with Mars's fiery energy.

These techniques and recipes provide a foundational approach to creating your own herbal preparations, tailored to the astrological influences that resonate most strongly with you. By incorporating these into your routine, you can enhance your physical, emotional, and spiritual health in alignment with the cosmic forces.

Appendix B: Astrological Timing for Herbal Work

Astrological timing can significantly enhance the potency and efficacy of herbal remedies by aligning their preparation and use with specific celestial energies. Understanding how to utilize planetary hours and days, as well as other astrological considerations, can deepen your herbal practice, connecting it more intimately with the rhythms of the cosmos.

Planetary Hours and Days

Planetary hours and days are ancient systems of timing that associate specific hours and days of the week with particular planets, each offering unique energies for various activities, including herbal work.

1. **Understanding Planetary Days:**

Each day of the week is ruled by a different planet, influencing the types of activities best suited for those days:

- **Sunday (Sun):** Ideal for preparing herbs that promote health, vitality, and success.
- **Monday (Moon):** Best for working with herbs related to emotional healing, psychic awareness, and fertility.
- **Tuesday (Mars):** Suitable for concocting remedies that boost energy, protection, and courage.
- **Wednesday (Mercury):** Optimal for remedies involving communication, intellect, and travel.
- **Thursday (Jupiter):** Good for expanding knowledge, legal matters, and prosperity.
- **Friday (Venus):** Perfect for creating beauty treatments, love potions, and harmony blends.
- **Saturday (Saturn):** Ideal for formulations that focus on structure, discipline, and longevity.

2. **Utilizing Planetary Hours:**

Planetary hours are calculated based on the time of sunrise and sunset, with each hour of the day and night being governed by a different planet in a specific order. Here's how to harness these hours:

- **Calculate planetary hours:** Determine the time of sunrise and sunset in your location. Divide the daytime and nighttime into twelve equal parts; each part is a planetary hour.
- **Select appropriate hours:** Choose hours ruled by a planet that corresponds to the energy you wish to imbue in your herb. For instance, prepare a love tincture during the hour of Venus.

Astrological Considerations

Beyond planetary days and hours, other astrological events can influence herbal practices.

1. **Moon Phases:**

The phase of the Moon can affect plant growth and the potency of herbal remedies:

- **New Moon**: Ideal for starting new projects or remedies that require growth and increase.
- **Waxing Moon**: Good for formulating remedies that require accumulation, such as tonics for building up the body.
- **Full Moon**: Optimal for charging water and other preparations with lunar energy, perfect for peak potency.
- **Waning Moon**: Best for making remedies aimed at reduction, such as weight loss aids or detoxification blends.

2. **Planetary Alignments and Retrogrades:**

Paying attention to planetary alignments (such as conjunctions, trines, and oppositions) and retrogrades can also enhance your herbal work:

- **Alignments**: Use alignments for synergistic effects, such as Jupiter and Sun for expansion and success, or Venus and Moon for emotional balancing and beauty.
- **Retrogrades**: Prepare remedies that counteract the challenges associated with retrogrades, such as Mercury retrograde (communication issues) or Mars retrograde (low energy and aggression).

3. **Eclipses:**

Eclipses are powerful times for transformation. Herbal work done during an eclipse can be particularly potent for initiating deep change. However, it is advised to be aware of the intense energies and use them wisely.

Conclusion

Incorporating astrological timing into your herbal practices not only aligns your work with the natural energies of the universe but also enhances the effectiveness and specificity of your herbal remedies. By carefully considering planetary hours, days, and significant astrological events, you can maximize the healing and transformative power of your herbal preparations. This knowledge serves as a valuable tool in the art and science of astrological herbalism, bridging the celestial and the earthly in your quest for wellness and spiritual growth.

Message from the Author:

I hope you enjoyed this book, I love astrology and knew there was not a book such as this out on the shelf. I love metaphysical items as well. Please check out my other books:

-Life of Government Benefits

-My life of Hell

-My life with Hydrocephalus

-Red Sky

-World Domination:Woman's rule

-World Domination:Woman's Rule 2: The War

-Life and Banishment of Apophis: book 1

-The Kidney Friendly Diet

-The Ultimate Hemp Cookbook

-Creating a Dispensary(legally)

-Cleanliness throughout life: the importance of showering from childhood to adulthood.

-Strong Roots: The Risks of Overcoddling children

-Hemp Horoscopes: Cosmic Insights and Earthly Healing

- Celestial Hemp Navigating the Zodiac: Through the Green Cosmos

-Astrological Hemp: Aligning The Stars with Earth's Ancient Herb

-The Astrological Guide to Hemp: Stars, Signs, and Sacred Leaves

-Green Growth: Innovative Marketing Strategies for your Hemp Products and Dispensary

-Cosmic Cannabis

-Astrological Munchies

-Henry The Hemp

-Zodiacal Roots: The Astrological Soul Of Hemp

- Green Constellations: Intersection of Hemp and Zodiac

-Hemp in The Houses: An astrological Adventure Through The Cannabis Galaxy

-Galactic Ganja Guide

Heavenly Hemp

Zodiac Leaves

Doctor Who Astrology

Cannastrology

Stellar Satvias and Cosmic Indicas

Celestial Cannabis: A Zodiac Journey

AstroHerbology: The Sky and The Soil: Volume 1

AstroHerbology:Celestial Cannabis:Volume 2

Cosmic Cannabis Cultivation

The Starry Guide to Herbal Harmony: Volume 1

The Starry Guide to Herbal Harmony: Cannabis Universe: Volume 2

Yugioh Astrology: Astrological Guide to Deck, Duels and more

Nightmare Mansion: Echoes of The Abyss

Nightmare Mansion 2: Legacy of Shadows

Nightmare Mansion 3: Shadows of the Forgotten

Nightmare Mansion 4: Echoes of the Damned

The Life and Banishment of Apophis: Book 2

Nightmare Mansion: Halls of Despair

Healing with Herb: Cannabis and Hydrocephalus

Check out my Virtual dispensary for all your hemp needs: https://shift.store/sg1fan23477/retail

If you want solar for your home go here: https://www.harborsolar.live/apophisenterprises/
Instagrams:
@apophis_enterprises,
@hempkingdom2024,
@apophisbookemporium,
@apophisfashion,
@apophisscardshop
Twitter: @apophisenterpr1,
Tiktok:@apophisenterprise
Youtube: @sg1fan23477
Podcast: Apophis Chat Zone: https://open.spotify.com/show/5zXbrCLEV2xzCp8ybrfHsk?si=fb4d4fdbdce44dec
Newsletter: https://apophiss-newsletter-27c897.beehiiv.com/